broken beauty

pov - a breakup:

for the little miss overthinkers

by echo ㅈ

POV - A BREAKUP:
FOR THE LITTLE MISS OVERTHINKERS

ISBN: 979-8-218-47613-7 (paperback)

Layout Design and Illustrations by: Rein G.
www.fiverr.com/reindrawthings

to all the little miss overthinkers out there,
going through heartbreak:

there is beauty in the madness.

preface

this book is for all the girls out there
going through heartbreak
who are their own
little miss overthinkers,

whose minds spiral
into endless questioning,
and self-torturing,
and what-ifs.

if no one has ever
told you,

i hope you know that
your brain,

your overthinking,
perhaps a bit
self-destructive,
ever-analyzing mind,
is beautiful.

and i hope
you find
that this book
is a place

to find
beauty
in the madness
of a mind
of a little miss overthinker

for the days when...

you've just
broken up

you were my maybe
i knew from the start,

but i never really thought
you'd one day break my heart.

i woke up today
and my heart was dead inside,

so i pushed it away
i've got no use for it
not anymore, anyways.

one
two,
buckled my shoes.

three
four,
went out the door

five
six,
bought brownie mix

seven
eight,
wondered how long it'd take,

for me to stop counting
each time my lungs i n f l a t e.

weeping red

sometimes the universe
seems frozen in time;

a static painting
whose colors begin to unwind.

for the world is no more
than a blend of pigment

with malicious hues that swim,
colliding in the sky.

~ and so the stars begin to melt
trickling through the sky,

shimmery tears of gold
for the birds to fly by.

~ and the sun is plummeting
down into the sea

as shades of fiery yellow
clash -
- with a cerulean syncope.

~ and the ground seems to shudder
convulse under our feet,

and its earthy tones
intertwine,
with the sky's
lonely retreat.

and once all the world
had dissolved

and a painting,
a muddle,
of what an artist had once known,

then our heart would follow -

- bleeding
out
into
smoke

weeping
red.

just keep breathing
just keep breathing.

**you start
to miss him**

the nights seem colder
since you've gone

i turn up the heater,
but the cold remains.

my heater is no replacement
for the warmth of the sun.

glass slippers

i look for you
you know?

i look for you
in the thousands
of pieces
of cinderella's glass slipper,

our happily ever after
crushed
under our bleeding feet.

would it be
too much
to
ask if
we could
stare
into the
mirror
for
days on end,

and see ourselves
dancing, my
velvet skirts

clashing
against your,
navy-gray
suit,

lights
darkened
like the acid
poured
onto the
stone ceiling?

or,
have i
imagined you
too?

**you see him again
for the first time**

number games

if the world
was ending, and
24 hours
was all
we had left,

would you,
finally,
run with me

through all the
even-ifs, and
leap
with me, across
all the odds?

Run,

i'd tell you,

run from the millions,
down to the thousands
and jump past the hundreds,

time's chasing at our heels:

you,
jump across the 1s, and 3s, and 5s, and 7s, and 9s

while i,
    follow,
        with the 2s and 4s and 6s
                        and 8s and 0s

you
were always so
good
at following
the rules.

and when
we'd finally reached
our last
24
hours,

i'd invert all
your commas, the
b r e a k s
in our sentences,
until,

we were
a quotation,

clingingtight
to each
other,

wondering

who made up
the rules,
to this
stupid
number game.

give and take

you left first.
your eyes wouldn't meet mine.

you rushed out of the hallway,
and only said
two words.

i guess the agony in my eyes
went
unheard.

i only wanted to hear your voice.
to see you
and speak to you,
as if fate had made a different choice.

but my one step forward
was your three back

my open eyes
met your passive gaze,

my two sentences
returned your two words

and my timid knock
left a closed door.

and so, im left

here

feeling small.

wondering how much i mattered,

if i did at all.

crosswalks

one day,
if i stood
at the other side
of our crosswalk,

would you travel
the bridge
of white
against gray,

and join me
in the middle -

- sinking,
suffocating,
in
black
concrete?

breakdown.

drowning in you

silence is loud
they said,

and so

with a silent scream

i drowned.

you never heard me.

drowning in us

what if one day
i dont
come up
for air,

and join the whales,

sinking
into
emptiness.

murder mystery

the most brutal homicide
is one
that kills
parts of you
you know
you will never
find.

**you just want
to be "friends".**

i wonder
why i even bother,

because it always seems
like each time i reach,

you only end up

f
  a
    r
      t
        h
          e
            r

from me.

placebo

i cannot
convince
this body,
this
soul,
that once knew
yours,

that the placebo
of our
friendship

can cure
this illness.

it knows.

acquaintances with the moon

if you will
not allow me
to
touch the sun

if you will
not allow
me
to weave
myself,

into the threads
of rays
coming undone,

i will fall
and fall
back
towards earth,

and
perhaps
i shall
have to
settle with

being
acquaintances,

with the
moon instead.

it hit you,
how much you love him

across the blue depths
we're drowning
irises fracturing
closing
each time
i blink

will you come
rescue me?

i reach out my hand,
but the waves
swallow me
down

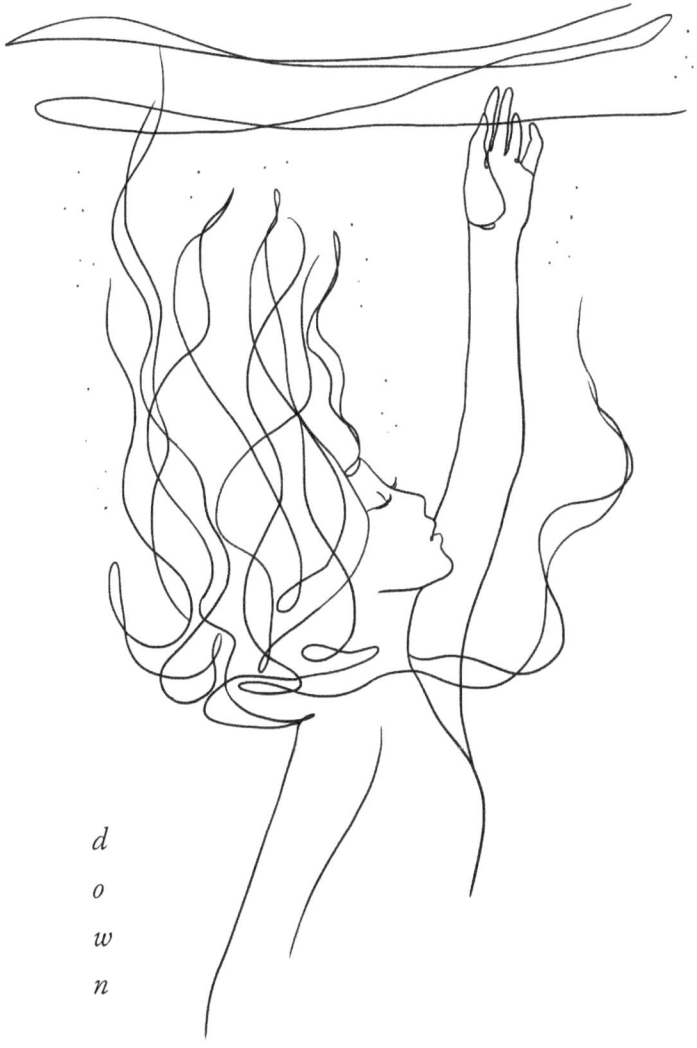

d
o
w
n

as you float
along the shore.

open your eyes.

love metaphor

love has already been expressed
in every possible way,
in every feasible manner
that a human can fathom to say.

compared to a flower,
or a midsummer's day.

the priceless value
of an unlived life
or the haunting beauty
of one twilight.

but love has never been expressed,
in the form of you.

love has never been told
about the folded corners
of your wise eyes,

and it has never been declared,
from the way your lips
curve slowly
when you smile.

love has never been conveyed
through the l e t t e r s of your name
but with the caveat
of how i once laid its claim.

and love,
love was never threaded;
through the memories
of me
and you.

i love you,

you, my infinitcly finite metaphor
for love.

earth elements

love was the air
you brought
into my lungs
at 3:14am
on a Tuesday morning,
as i was suffocating
in my head.

love was the fire
that you built me
camping -
- beside our special lake,
when the air was icy,
creeping through
my fingertips,
cold to chase the cold.

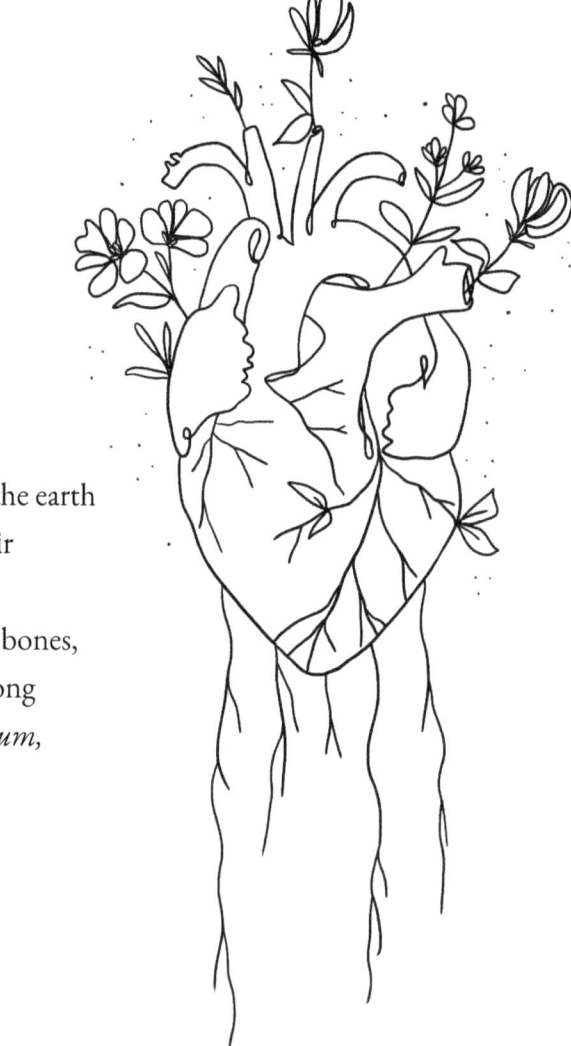

and love was the earth
of roots of hair
and the water
sprouting my bones,
heart beat strong
ba-dum, ba-dum,

Ba-dum.

life giver
death reaper
soul taker
mortal maker.

Immortality
of a mortal lover.

an unconventional
conventional love

if someone had asked
me
to tell them
about love

i would skip
past the Keat moon
and beauty
of falling stars,

i would leap across
the great waters
blue depths
of the Shelly sea,

i would climb
past the vines
of the gardens,

Shakespeare's roses
petals,
under my feet

and i'd jump the flames
dancing
dancing
around the Austen fire,

to love
is to burn
to love
is to burn

and instead,
i would take them,

past the constellations
35, 27, 16
freckles
lining your back
across the blue depths
drowning
irises fracturing
closing
each time
you blink

climb the roots
up the stems
blossoms
in your hair,

and dive,
engulfed
by the flames
hot
sickly sweet
when you kissed me,
january 17th,
one cold evening.

no,
love is not conventional.

love is my own poetry,
found,
scrawled
in your skin.

someone else
likes him

yet the love in my heart
fell like a stone,
dropped from the sky
and crushed my bones,

and it doubled and tripled
until i couldn't take its weight,

and it doubled and tripled
and felt like a mistake,

then i realised,
i understood why;

your sun had once held my sky.

and so i knew
that one day,

maybe from
your memory,
i'd fade away.

perhaps id be
but a small piece,

and that's okay.

for ill remember.

have you ever
heard
about the
mirror,
the mirror
of
three
dimensions?

send light
off one,
and it blinds
the second,
send light
off the second,
and it sparks
the
third.

reflect
and refract
and bend
and twist,

until,

each dimension
is
painted
in those,
particular
wavelengths
of light.

perhaps my
colors
do not shine
as brightly
as hers.

he left you
on read

drowning in air (2)

silence is loud
they said,

and so

with a silent scream

i drowned.

i hope no one hears me.

sure,
let's play.

let's play this
stupid
game,

where the minutes
of silence
are the points
in the round,

and the winner
is the one
who uses
the least
letters.

let's scrabble
this thing,

and score
doubles
and triples,

right painful words
at the right *freaking* time.

i think,

i don't want to
play
anymore.

i just
never knew
that
my all
would seep
into
your nothingness.

did i ever really exist,
to you?

or was i simply

a *figment*
of your imagination,

bent
and *twisted*
and *stretched*

only to disappear,

be discarded
and
cast away,

once i no longer fit

within the confines -

- of your imagination?

you change
your hair

if i cut
my hair,

would the
roots
of stems
and blossoms
of yours,

be cut off
too?

snip

if only the heart
was like our hair;
a pair of scissors
and cut were all our cares.

for the fragments of you
are braided into my soul;

and so i'd snip.

cut off the beach-soiled strands
from those summer nights,
where we laid in the sand
until the late sunrise.

and i'd snip.

trim off those fibers
still scented by steak,
when i had wanted to pay
on our very first date.

and i'd snip.

tear out those tendrils
that brushed your shoulder,
when i first held your hand
and the season was colder.

and i'd snip,
and snip
and

s
 n
  i
   p

until

i was standing
in a pile of our memories

and i'd look at myself in the mirror
and say,

new roots shall grow from today.

maybe you're getting over him.

embroidery

if all i have
left of you
is this *single*
thread,

at least
it will sew
me together,
long enough

for me
to re embroider
my heart
in black
and blue
instead.

letter 0.5, xoxo

i want you to go.

but i don't.

it's weird,

i want you to stay,
only so i can tell you to leave.

i want you to go,
because maybe
i don't have the strength
to tell you to leave.

now that i finally have the strength,
the strength
that's pushing you
shoving you,
out of
my head,

maybe i don't want
the strength
to *want* this
at all.

then again,
it was always very simple.

i always wanted you
to want me.

pretty lies

pretty words
spoken
one summer day,

melting
down
the
sky

as the sun
fades
away.

that one song starts
to play

repeat

a wall around my heart
a fortress around my soul,
a cage
so as to not

let
my
feelings
come
apart.

headphones in my ear
and phone in hand,

and i'll press play.

and i'll drown out the world
with whatever it takes,

and i'll drown out his smile
with a slice of chocolate cake.

and i'll drown out the echoes
of past and present

and i'll drown out the memories -
and beat back a lover's disease.

until

the drum of the rhythm
starts it's entreat,
yet the tempo somehow seems
incomplete;

missing the cadence
of his slow heartbeat.
until the first notes of the song
are strummed in secret,

yet lacking the timbre
that his voice emits.

until the chorus of lyrics
break the flow of the wind,
and the memories come rushing;
so from reality you abscind.

and you press repeat.

and you remember the feel
of his hand in yours,

and you remember the conversations
where your dreams were explored

and you press repeat.

and you remember the time
he told you he loved you,

and you remember his soul,
the one enigma you adored

and
you
press
repeat.

until the melodies of song
are drowned out
by the melodies of antiquity;
where once two hearts
walked their lonely route.

and you press repeat.

and the tempo runs wild,
the lyrics defiled
and the notes are beguiled
by one's artistries
of a missing soul.

and the chords of that song
shall clash with your own,
the melody of a pop rhapsody,
and the ecstasy two hearts have sewn.

and you'll press repeat
and you'll press repeat

and
you'll
press
repeat.

until your heart realizes
that the composition of this song
was only meant to have one author,
never two, only one.

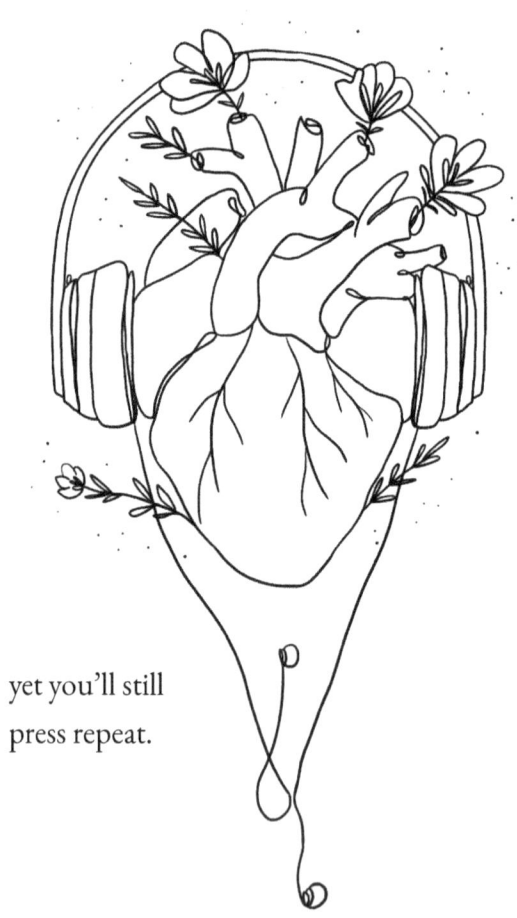

yet you'll still
press repeat.

you're back
to loving him

and *still*
i loved
like truths
so *blind*

and still i loved,
my feelings ruling my mind.

terra firma antithesis

maybe it's selfish
that i wanted
your rain

as i watched you
flowing freely
across the sky

while i was
stuck,
embedded

in soil
of roots
in shoes
of stems
of feet,

planted
in
time

watching.

no matter where you are
or,
the places of our scars,

no matter the distance
of whatever ocean
between us,

the love we harboured,
bleeds through my existence.

i love you.

oxygen deficient

can you feel
my heart
beating?
thrumming,

under
your fingertips
pounding
badum badum
badum

no,
don't move,

let my veins
absorb
your oxygen

arteries root
veins

let them twine,
fuse
together

our bodies,
our oxygen.

i think,
i have run out of air.

he might like
another girl

melting rainbows

i'll try to
ignore
the way, that
you
look at
her.

the way, that
your right hand
trembles,
like it
itches,
to tuck that
strand
behind her ear.

don't worry,
i'll ignore
the way,
red tints the
edges of
my eyes,

i see
red,

i see maroon;
To love
is to
Burn.

the ground is
fissuring
beneath me,

and i see, myself
swallowed
whole
by those
bleeding
fissures.

and i am bleeding
in black and blue and red and green
and yellow and orange and purple too,

melting rainbows
falling out of the sky.

from here,
ill remember
from here,
 ill recall

ill hold our secrets,
even as i stand small.

ill remember.

as *you* slowly forget.

you found something that belonged to him

why does
the universe
do this?

sure,
let's just
throw a meteor
at a
collapsing
star.

stretch the gray
t-shirt,
over
my head.

feel as the
cotton threads
poke
and pull, and
yank at my skin

i never understood
why you, you liked
this t-shirt.

it was
it was
always too
light
gray, too
rough.

like dragging rough
weeds,
across my skin.

i look at myself
in the mirror.

the fabric
tinted
a darker gray,
cotton softened,
soaked, by
tears.

i cut it up into pieces.

take it back.
i don't want it.

i don't *want*
to want it.

another
lonely night

midnight dreams

sometimes i sit
by my candlelight
and dream of a world
where shadows come to life.

where the darkness
is no longer
my only friend
and your warmth
embraces me instead.

where the silence of night
does not drown me
in suffocating air
but keeps secrets
of your hands -
- tangled in my hair.

where the howling winds
of a cold winter night
fades

against the hot summer storm
of you
and i.

but as the moon
hangs
from the sky
and the comets
fall
colliding as the fly,

the cold envelopes me
and darkness embraces me

for the clock ticks
midnight,

and my dream
has been washed away.

xoxo, dreams of a nightmare

once upon a time,
there lived a girl,
and this girl -
- she met a boy.

the girl was in love
with books,
with the worlds
she would only ever dream of.

this girl was in love
with living a thousand lives
through each author's eyes,
writing herself into fantasy -
- round and round the web she went.

and the boy was a world
the girl had never known.

for even after
all the tales she'd read,

the boy was
of another sort
all together;

the girl
could reach out her hand,
and for the first time,
a hand would reach out
in return.

and so,
the girl fell in love
with the boy,
the boy
with the holdable hands.

and the girl

loved the boy,
so much so
that she gifted him
her pen.

and before long,
the boy began
to write her stories,

each one
spinning threads -
- around and around
her spider's web.

—

but before long,
the boy began
to rewrite history,

circle
criss cross
strike through
underline

and before long,
the pen
ran out of ink,
and the boy decided
he was tired
of writing.

and so,
left was the girl
in her unfinished story
of pretty lies,

the bitter fantasy
left behind
for the next author.

i never thought i'd be here,
still broken over you.

letter 1, xoxo

yes,
i've been ignoring you.

yes,
i pretend like you don't exist.

but that's not because i don't love you.
that's not because i've gotten over you.

reality is the cold truth.

 and pretending is so much easier.

because to face reality would mean that in months,
i still think of you day and night.
to face reality would mean that when i think of you
with someone else, my soul shreds apart.
reality would mean that you might have gotten over me,
but i *still* have not.

i still hunger for your presence,
the connection of our hearts.

and i hear the whispers from those around me
there's better out there,

just move on,
breathe,
and you'll see.

yet,
it's been so many months,
and you still surround me.

you think you've loved
him for too long

embroidery 2

i suppose
my heart
must first
learn
to stitch itself
together

before
it can embroider
our initials,

our letters
across
their sentences.

letter 2, xoxo

i promised myself that i would be over you by now.
its funny, its been what feels like a lifetime,
and i still think about you.

i wake up, and you're on my mind,
i ride the bus, you're on my mind,
i go to bed, you're on my mind.

i don't know how its possible to have loved
someone so much,
and i don't know whether i still love you.

i think a part of me will always love you,
whether or not we're together.

i havent talked to you in months, weeks and days.
but you're still on my mind every month,
every week, and every day.

i want to talk to you, i want to see you smile,
hear you laugh.
i want to know what it feels like to embrace
your warmth.

i want you to be mine, and me to be yours.

and it feels like we're still playing a game,
a game i thought i ended when i sent you
that last message.

to see who can care less
to see who has more friends
to see who is doing better.

i just wanted you to know,
that it *kills* me,
to ignore you.
to pretend you don't exist.

it *kills* my heart
and my soul,
but my head is yelling at me.
screaming,

that this fickle thing we call love
has *hurt* me.

that this fickle thing we call love,
is not as important as grades, as school,
as university,

and everyone says thats right;
and maybe it is.

i'm not going to lie,
sometimes i wish,
selfishly,
that you're struggling just as i am.

and i'm not going to lie,
i want you to see how apathetic i can pretend to be,
because selfishly,
i want you to think well of me.

and i'm not going to lie,
sometimes i get jealous
of those who can talk to you as they wish,
feel your presence in their midst.

although i have no right.

you'll probably never think this of me.
although my heart secretly wishes you might.

what i wouldn't give to have just one conversation
with no consequence;

with all walls down,
and open doors.

i would ask you how you've been,
and whether you're okay.
i would ask you whether you loved me,
although i convince myself you did.

i would ask you whether you still care for me,
as i do you,

and if so,
if we could return to being best friends;
who carried each other's hearts.

but that is a fantasy,
because even as my heart hopes,
my head is what has never failed me,
in this world's reality.

so i wish you,
everything,

even though i heartbrokenly
wish you nothing,
all the same.

god,
thinking your name hurts.

at least i can tell you what you
once wanted to hear;
thank you for being my first love.

i love you.

seasonal lovers

for as much as
summer
holds tight
to its flowery
buds, and
blue skies,

fall
paints itself
in vivacious hues
of red and
orange

and a creeping
suspicion,
as fall peers
between the
leaves
of one maple
tree,

quiet longing
for the
warmth
of summer's
hand,

to reach, and
perhaps brush
the rays, of
silky sunlit
strands,

tumbling
down
her back.

but the leaves,
they must
fall
and the
time must
pass.

summer never stays.

the time has come,
to bid you farewell.

to close this chapter,
before my heart can rebel.

you finally
give him up

love flame   *to love*
flickering   *is to burn*
fighting,   *to love*
against the wind   *is to burn*

heart candle   *to love*
burning,   *to burn*
wax seal   *to love*
stamped   *to burn*
into our skin

                                               love
                                               to burn

and as for you and i,

                                               love
                                               burn,

we dance,
dance   no.
around
around   love,
Austen's flame,   love was
calling,   never
chanting,   immortal.

heart anatomy

my heart is still coated
with reminders of you

like a glaze of syrup
sweet but sticky
honeydew.

it pumps through my arteries
and back through my veins

infuses every bone
drills through every muscle.

So

i'll re-oxygenate my blood
and treat its remission,
till my veins are no longer filled
with your resuscitation

and i'll put back up the walls
that your presence knocked down,
separating mind from matter
three cardiums let drown.

and i'll force it to beat
coerce it to pulse
and this new heart will flutter
and clean veins convulse

and that sticky honeydew
shall be wiped away
only to leave
a wistful residue.

i can
feel myself
coming back
in waves,

stronger and
stronger.

the tide is
rising, and

come
high tide,

and i will
wash you
away.

you want to give up on love

i never
feared
all that
you were,

instead,
i feared
that it would disappear,

into our
nothingness.

all or nothing

all
or nothing
you said,

as you kissed my scars

all
or nothing
you said,

as you traced my wounds

give me all
or nothing,
you said.

and so i poured
and poured
myself
into you:

as your kisses
left blood
staining
my skin

as you *touched* me -
- the brush
of your skin
on mine

as you healed
some wounds
but left death
trailing
in its wake.

you killed parts
of me
i know
i will never find.

quantum entanglement

no.
don't move,
please.

is it
is it
even possible
that you,
you don't feel
the instantaneous
connection,

this dance, between
you and i?

wait.
please.

please don't leave.

please
let me,
let me
dance,

dance with
you
in our quantum
symphony.

let us
dance.

we were the
paradox, of
schrödinger's
love,

we were,
we were
alive,
with immeasurable
possibility.

we were the
immeasurable,
we were, the
unobserved.

we were what
no author
may perfectly
write,
no singer
wholly
lyricize.

in the
quantum-entanglement
of hearts,

we were love,
written in the language
of an infinite
equation.

~

now, as
our entanglement
fades, and
the universe
recalibrates,

even in the
infinite, the undefined,
i find no answers.

black lace

i wont ask
what happened
to forever,

as long as i know
i was
one moment

embroidered
in lace
among
your stars.

and now,

now i
fly
carried by the wind,

off to the earth
of the *immortalized*
mortals.

a new era

and i see the bridge

i've been walking for minutes
and hours
and days
and months
and perhaps years,

dreaming of the next universe,
for its path to appear.

and i've wished
for this next world,
where i leave behind
the heartache of this planet's toil.

and so i've traveled,

through the forest of memories
the desert of lonely beings

swam through
coral reefs of lover's disease

and past the volcanoes;
heavy ashes of suffocating jealousy.

ive climbed the tundras
of distance and freeze,
and scaled the mountains
of senseless complexity.

yet for all of my travels
and all of this mortal's esthete,
i've remained trapped
sweltered by the biomes of this reality,
but now i see the bridge.

and i can see the divide
the wondrous swirling colors,
colliding in the sky

and i can see the partings of tide
the tinges of blue
separating time and space,
and i spot the flying meteor that signifies

a new age
and era
and time has arrived.

and i see the bridge.

darling,
you are your own
poetry.

dear future me,

i fear that all
i am
is not enough
for all
i was meant
to be.

poem one: the urge to be loved

like the sea.

to be fondled within its dark depths
and be called
desired

like a comet

to be held throughout a dark sky
and be called
wanted

like the air.

to be named the source to a world
and be called

life.

to crave touch
to want tenderness
to desire to feel

be loved as melancholy loves memory
and sonder may love the strange

poem two: to be loved

like the sea.

to be caressed by its shallow waters
and be called
coveted

like a comet.

to soar brilliantly through the navy sky
and be called
immortal.

like the air.

to find the air in your world
and let it be called

everlasting.

to be touched
tunderstand tenderness
to feel what others feel

be as memory, as it once loved melancholy
but how strange; you have realized sonder.

a goodbye

if the sun was fire, i'd be rain

if the sun was fire
i'd be rain

for from desire of relief
i'd abstain,

and to my soul
i'd bid farewell

long before
the lies we'd tell.

the night you burned
and lit the sky,

my end had come
- the ocean all dry.

the stars had fallen
down dripped the moon,

melting away,`
midnight struck soon.

thank the world for the life,
the life,

we breathed.

i wish you love
i wish you peace.

i wish you a forever,

though
not
with
me.

and,
as for that small piece
that you have of me,

i hope you'll keep it
yet set us free.

but we loved like the seasons
all throughout the years.

we loved
like the tide,
broken forevers,
shall always fly.

and ill remember,
from the earth,
and to heaven,

always and forever.

you've reached me,
_____,
you've reached me.

the wild girl

and she was running,
running
running

from the chasing hounds, from the / weeping
willows // and the / shadowy alcoves

dear earth,
shall you ever find her?

locks of brown hair / stretching out, //
twisting / tumbling / arching, //
branches of / what was / so profoundly /
humanly, // her.

blossoming / and breathless,
she touched / the sky //
clouds / forming wings, wind / forming
breath, / bleeding blue into blue

dear heaven,
shall you ever find her?

and she bent / and folded / and broke, //
ripping the stratosphere / viciously /
tearing through the / clouds,

an ode to the sky.

and the will'o'whisps / sang //
lovely child,
this is metamorphosis.

my dear mortality,
shall you ever find me?

acknowledgements

there is a very long list of people who have inspired this book,
and will likely never know of its existence.

but i'd still like to thank all of them,
the friends, the family,
and the first teenage love
who still holds parts of me.

there are, however, some people who know about,
who experienced,
the overthinking, the struggles, and heartache,
that went into the creation of this book.

i'd like to thank them, as well. *(name order is alphabetical)*

~

ara c. - same person, different font.
i hope that life takes you where you wish to go,
and that you realise that something lost to you,
something you search for but cannot find,
is always found.

never lose yourself,
you are divinely special.

~

elze s. - you are my beautifully real person, in a terribly fake world.

ever heard that one before?

either way, i know you will find your peace, because you have been that for me.

and you,

so terrifyingly,

and beautifully strong,

you will forge your own way.

~

family - if i had the power to choose what family i wanted to be born into,

i would still choose this one, every time.

thank you for putting up with the endless overthinking, and rants, and everything.

~

jenny m. - one of the most hauntingly beautiful minds, i have ever seen.

i hope you find all that your soul is looking for,

in both yourself, and the world.

everything you want for yourself, you just have to find.
i have no doubt that for someone like you,
it's just out there,

waiting.

~

j,p, - you might never know this exists,
or perhaps you will,
but i'd like to say that i'm truly grateful.

i hope you live a wondrous life,
and thank you.

~

laura k. - another beautiful mind.
i am so grateful to have been able to learn from yours.
the workings of my mind have been inspired by yours.

about echo ㅈ

yes, it is a pseudonym.
no, you may not know my real name.

yes, i am an overthinker.

i loved writing since i was very young.
tried writing my first novel at age 11.
published it,
it didn't go so well.

lives in korea currently, but will likely be
moving to the u.s. soon.
aside from reading and writing,
i love to read philosophy,
and watch horror movies.

socials ~

📷 @littlemissoverthinker

📌 littemissoverthinker

broken
beauty,
flourishing

www.ingramcontent.com/pod-product-compliance
Lightning Source LLC
Chambersburg PA
CBHW061803120626
46550CB00005B/2118